999 Bucket List Ideas for Couples
Fun & Romantic Things To Do With Your Boo

EnzBzty

© **Copyright 2020 - All rights reserved.**

The content contained within this book may not be reproduced, duplicated or transmitted without direct written permission from the author or the publisher.

Under no circumstances will any blame or legal responsibility be held against the publisher, or author, for any damages, reparation, or monetary loss due to the information contained within this book, either directly or indirectly.

Legal Notice:

This book is copyright protected. It is only for personal use. You cannot amend, distribute, sell, use, quote or paraphrase any part, or the content within this book, without the consent of the author or publisher.

Disclaimer Notice:

Please note the information contained within this document is for educational and entertainment purposes only. All effort has been executed to present accurate, up to date, reliable, complete information. No warranties of any kind are declared or implied. Readers acknowledge that the author is not engaged in the rendering of legal, financial, medical or professional advice. The content within this book has been derived from various sources. Please consult a licensed professional before attempting any techniques outlined in this book.

By reading this document, the reader agrees that under no circumstances is the author responsible for any losses, direct or indirect, that are incurred as a result of the use of the information contained within this document, including, but not limited to, errors, omissions, or inaccuracies.

1. Go on a trip somewhere you've never been.

2. Mail a handwritten letter to each other.

3. Rent a super luxurious Airbnb for one night together.

4. Brew your own coffee together.

5. Cuddle on the rooftop.

6. Watch the sunrise together (with #5)

7. Watch the sunset together (again, preferably with #5)

8. Take couples' pictures in a photo booth.

9 Tell each other one secret you've never shared.

10 Binge watch a new show.

11 Host the best dinner party of your lives together.

12 Rush into a taxi together and yell "follow that car!"

13 Tour a Scandinavian country (or countries) together.

14 Camp under the Aurora (northern lights).

15 Buy your dream apartment together.

16 Write a heartfelt love letter to each other.

25. Plan a movie night to watch each other's favorite films together.

26. Find the best double date partners and tag along.

27. Stay up all night cuddling and talking.

28. Build a cozy pillow fort.

29. Kiss in the rain – The Notebook style.

30. Spend an entire Sunday in bed together without phones.

31. Create your own board game together.

32. Have an in-home spa day, and give each other massages.

17. Revisit your first-kiss spot.

18. Kiss on your first-kiss spot.

19. Have an "our song."

20. Have an "our dance."

21. Get a polaroid camera to capture your special moments.

22. Stay in a Maldives overwater bungalow.

23. Have breakfast in bed together at a fancy hotel.

24. Go overboard on your significant other's next birthday surprise.

33 Go for a luxurious couples' massage.

34 Plan an entirely tech-free date with your partner.

35 Learn a new party trick together.

36 Try couple's yoga for the first time.

37 Plan your future together, and write down ideas.

38 Meet each other's families.

39 Grow a flower plant together.

40 Grow a garden together and eat its fresh produce.

41 Go for scuba diving together.

42 Have a bake-off.

43 Go on an adventure.

44 Make a memorable vlog out of it.

45 Surprise your partner by cooking their favorite meal for dinner.

46 Have a couples-only bonfire.

47 Play a Mr. and Mrs. game of truth or strip.

48 Play hide and seek at an Ikea near you.

49 Draw each other and frame it – no matter how bad it is.

50 Skydive together!

51 Dance in the rain.

52 Go berry picking together.

53 Have a private book club with your partner, and read along with them.

54 Go on a romantic picnic.

55 Build a snowman, name him, and take pictures with him!

56 Jump together in a pile of fresh autumn leaves.

57 Paddle around a lake in a rowboat – just the two of you.

58 Host the best game night together for your friends and family.

59 Go on a dreamy hot air balloon ride together!

60 Have dinner on the balcony, with a stunning night view.

61 Visit a museum together.

62 Volunteer and do something good for your community together.

63 Ice skate together!

64 Have a go-carting date.

65. Make a pizza together!

66. Bake cookies together.

67. Swim with the whale sharks with your partner.

68. Visit an ancient spot together.

69. Admire the art of renaissance in Florence.

70. Go on a long, unforgettable road trip.

71. Visit Disneyland.

72. Write down and conquer your biggest fears together.

73. Go bungee jumping as a couple.

74. Have a beach picnic together.

75. Fly first class with your partner.

76. Go on a long drive out of town.

77. Walk on the great wall of China.

78. Visit the Pyramids of Giza.

79. Tour Japan and learn their culture together.

80. Have a one-month stay in the city of Prague.

81 Kiss under the Eiffel tower.

82 Experience a camel ride together.

83 Explore and dive into Iceland's Blue Lagoon.

84 Admire the Grand Canyon together.

85 Visit the Canadian Niagara Falls together.

86 Party together in Ibiza!

87 Float down the heavenly Amazon River in a boat with your partner.

88 Watch the iconic Isla de Santorini sunset together.

89 Visit Cancun, and the ancient ruins within it.

90 Take a trip to Rio during the annual carnival.

91 Have an overnight stay at an ice hotel.

92 Get lost in Romantic Rome together!

93 Toss a coin into Rome's iconic Trevi Fountain.

94 Go exploring through a rainforest together.

95 Swing together 'at the end of the world' in Ecuador.

96 Learn sailing together.

97 Have a cozy group hug with a Panda, Koala, or Sloth.

98 Visit Dubai and skydive over The Palm together.

99 Go on a Desert Safari in the UAE.

100 Kiss on top of the Burj Khalifa.

101 Visit Dubai's iconic aquarium and underwater zoo.

102 Go on a cruise escape with your partner.

103 Hit the titanic pose together.

104 Experience an African safari together.

105 Attend the Oktoberfest in Munich.

106 Make an adventure bucket list.

107 Get on a game show together!

108 Go deep-sea fishing.

109 Take a helicopter ride over your city.

110 Fly in a private jet.

111 Watch the sunset from a volcano-top.

112 Beat an escape room as a team.

113 Go snorkeling.

114 Charter a yacht for one day.

115 Climb a huge mountain.

116 Ride horses together along the beach line.

117 Experience a total eclipse (with safety measures).

118 Learn a new language together.

119 Make your own language (made-up words only the two of you know).

120 Rent an RV and spend a night in it.

121 Visit a dreamy waterfall and let nature shower you!

122 Attend concerts of your favorite artists together.

123 Attend an over-the-top New Year's Eve celebration together.

124 Kiss your partner under fireworks.

125 Spend a day/night in a treehouse.

126 Camp on a mountain top overnight, and see the sunrise together.

127 Overcome physical challenges together!

128 Run a 5K marathon together.

129 Attend a huge sports match together.

130 Visit each other's hometowns – see where both of you grew up.

131 Take cooking classes together.

132 Take salsa classes together.

133 Revisit your first ever date – recreate and do the same stuff.

134 Have a romantic photoshoot done by a professional.

135 Write a poem for each other.

136 Tell each other five things you love about each other.

137 Help your partner heal through a sickness.

138 Adopt an adorable pet from a shelter home.

139 Have a stargazing night on your rooftop.

140 Eat strawberries with Nutella together.

141 Cuddle in a hammock together.

142 Hold hands and wander through a beautiful garden barefoot.

143 Have a candlelight dinner.

144 Learn to fly kites together.

145 Share an ice-cream.

146 Relax together in a hot tub or pool.

147 Visit an amusement park, and try all the rides.

148 Visit an arcade and win each other memorable gifts.

149 Make delicious s'mores for each other.

150 Experience a drive-in cinema for the first time.

151 Play Among Us together.

152 Try a new dish together.

153 Make a new dish together.

154 Shop for groceries together.

155 Go to the library together.

156 Play the "how well do you know each other?" trivia.

157 Attend comedy shows.

158 Do a DIY project together.

159 Set a budget and shop for each other.

160 Try bathing together (it saves water!)

161 Visit a park nearby.

162 Try each other's favorite ice cream flavor.

163 Karaoke together.

164 Watch YouTube videos together.

165 Listen to each other's favorite song.

166 Take cute selfies together.

167 Play FIFA together
(give each other a kiss for every goal!)

168 Wear each other's clothes.

1000 Bucket List Ideas for Couple

169 Make a playlist together.

170 Have a nap time together.

171 Have a meal on one plate.

172 Try naked cuddling.

173 Run errands together.

174 Paint a room together.

175 Have a Boba tea date!

176 Go to a workshop together.

177. Get some thrift shopping done together.

178. Visit a fancy restaurant.

179. Fake a proposal at a public place.

180. Visit an art gallery.

181. Draw together.

182. Build a sandcastle together.

183. Fake a birthday at a restaurant to get a free dessert.

184. Prank call people together.

185 Get each other a promise ring.

186 Meet each other's friends.

187 Spill the tea and gossip together.

188 Get a cute plushy together.

189 Go to a mall and chat about random things.

190 Watch horror movies together.

191 Go to a hard rock concert.

192 Do each other's makeup (get that eyeliner on fleek!)

193 Do each other's hair.

194 Visit an old bookstore together.

195 Online shop together.

196 Netflix and chill!

197 Make a fun TikTok video together.

198 Tie-dye old shirts together.

199 Do a face mask together.

200 Relieve your childhood and try activities you both enjoyed growing up.

201 Have a Photoshop war and edit each other's pictures.

202 Visit an animal shelter and play with fur babies.

203 Play dress up together.

204 Go on Omegle together.

205 Do a Q/A session on Instagram.

206 Wash each other's hair (Remember what Charles Boyle said?)

207 Solve a puzzle together.

208 Make a sandwich at Subway and then swap with each other.

209. Collect pretty rocks and shells for each other.

210. Have a Lego building date.

211. Do a comfort movie marathon.

212. Do the 4-course meals TikTok challenge.

213. Decorate your refrigerator with pictures and magnets.

214. Make a Pinterest board together.

215. Share your old photographs.

216. Have a Zoom or Skype date if you're away.

217. Watch "Try Not to Laugh" videos.

218. Job hunt together.

219. Shortlist universities together.

220. Look at cities you both would like to live in.

221. Make a bucket list.

222. Get your favorite pictures printed.

223. Try street food together.

224. Make out in a parking lot.

225 Spend the night at a hotel.

226 Have a Snapchat streak and be each other's Super BFF.

227 Reenact a scene from your favorite movie.

228 Share one blanket.

229 Go window shopping.

230 Buy a jewelry making kit.

231 Get a tattoo/piercing together.

232 Kiss each other under the moonlight.

233 Decorate your room with some fairy lights!

234 Visit a fortune teller and question regarding your future.

235 Read your horoscopes together.

236 Take silly Buzzfeed quizzes.

237 Video chat and cook/bake the same thing together.

238 Sleep on each other's shoulder during a train ride.

239 Buy flowers for each other.

240 Fall asleep on voice/video call together.

241 Have a work date.

242 Have a gingerbread house making competition.

243 Try roleplaying and act as your partner for a day.

244 Play Truth or Dare.

245 Go to a carnival together.

246 Tell each other embarrassing stories.

247 Share your worst date experiences.

248 Share your favorite date experiences.

249 Share your life's major inflection points.

250 Work out together.

251 Have an impromptu dance party.

252 Come up with creative business ideas.

253 Research ways to make business ideas happen.

254 Slow dance on a slow song together.

255 Go to a protest together.

256 Speak in a random accent for a day.

257 Watch movies with your mutual friends using Teleparty.

258 Read Wattpad stories together.

259 Watch highlights of old football games of your favorite teams.

260 Get a tent and camp indoors.

261 Go to every bakery in town and try one dessert per shop.

262 Paint on each other's backs.

263 Cut each other's hair.

264 Dye each other's hair the same color.

265 Visit a "worst-reviewed" restaurant.

266 Watch/read unsolved murder mysteries.

267 Watch old Vine compilations.

268 Jam to old Disney songs.

269 Watch serial killer documentaries together.

270 Go to a haunted house together.

271 Meet at a cute gazebo in a park.

272 Have a Podcast date (or make one together!)

273 Go on a bike ride together.

274 Watch a trashy reality TV show.

275 Follow a makeup tutorial together.

276 Do a FaceTime photo shoot if you're away.

277 Surprise each other with a scavenger hunt.

278 Have a bubble bath together.

279 Have a nerf gunfight.

280 Try the Kylie Jenner lip challenge.

281 Watch a movie in an XD cinema.

282 Visit historical places together.

283 Release floating lanterns (preferably biodegradable ones!)

284 Kiss each other underwater.

285 Make a scrapbook of your favorite memories.

286 Babysit together (if you both like kids).

287 Create an Instagram account together.

288 Make flower crowns together.

289 Catch lightning bugs.

290 Pick flowers and press them into books.

291 Show each other memes that make you laugh.

292 Go to a local fair and get your faces painted.

293 Paint each other's fingers and toenails.

294 Pick random ingredients and build a meal using them.

295 Visit a butterfly garden and count how many lands on you.

296 Tell each other ghost stories.

297 Write your names/initials on the beach.

298 Visit a little café by the sea.

299 Have a spicy food competition and see who drinks water first.

300 Wear ridiculous outfits outside and see how people react.

301 Lay on the grass together.

302 Make homemade ice cream.

303 Call while watching the same TV show/movie.

304 Read and discuss conspiracy theories.

305 Visit a food festival.

306 Visit a waterpark.

307 Attend/host a fancy-dress party.

308 Split a fancy milkshake.

309 Make each other a "Play Date" video edit.

310 Take a stroll at the zoo.

311 Visit the Taj Mahal.

312 Make some vases/pots in a pottery class together.

313 Have a paint fight.

314 Get a Netflix account together.

315 Take funny pictures together using Snapchat/Instagram filters.

316 Wear oversize unicorn pajamas and go out!

317 Try aerial yoga.

318 Decorate some cupcakes with your boo.

319 Get super dressed up and go to McDonald's.

320 Make fun of bad movies together.

321 Go hiking!

322 Go to a virtual reality arcade.

323 Declutter your closet and donate clothes.

324 Play 20 questions.

325 Play Charades and Pictionary.

326 Play "Never Have I Ever".

327 Play "Guess the Flavor".

328 Explore new ways of kissing.

329 Have a pillow fight!

330 Follow an unrealistic 5 Minutes Craft tutorial.

331 Discover old music.

332 Discover new artists.

333 Get a portrait made.

334 Watch anime together.

335 Dance with each other in the kitchen in the middle of the night.

336 Play The Sims and dress each other's avatar.

337 Redecorate your room together.

338 Have a conversation about whether you want kids.

339 Have a conversation about what you will name your kids.

340 Play Twister.

341 Come up with new cute names for each other.

342 Share a Disney inspired spaghetti kiss!

343 Kiss your partner on the top of the Ferris wheel.

344 Video call your mutual friends together.

345 Chase each other in public places.

346 Have a cooking competition.

347 Check the meaning of each other's names on Urban Dictionary.

348 Make separate folders for each other's pictures.

349 Try new hairstyles together.

350 Drive around during Christmas to look at lights/decorations.

351 Go shopping and push each other in a shopping cart.

352 Practice for interviews/presentations together.

353 Send each other random snaps on Snapchat.

354 Impersonate famous people.

355 Practice coffee art.

356 Recreate a dish created on MasterChef.

357 Make DIY scented candles.

358 Start your own traditions.

359 Feed the ducks.

360 Watch historical documentaries.

361 Share your dreams with each other.

362 Go through your Spotify discover weekly together.

363 Cook a meal from the leftovers in your refrigerator.

364 Watch a virtual concert.

365 Go to a fashion show together and rate the outfits.

366 Get each other a customized T-Shirt.

367 Have a water balloon fight (with food coloring).

368 Learn how to play an instrument together.

369 Read a romantic folk story.

370 Make drinks for each other.

371 Lay next to each other by a campfire.

372 Go to a playground together.

373 Try new cuisines.

374 Coordinate and wear matching outfits.

375 Make out in the back seat of your car.

376 Visit an abandoned house together.

377 If you're away, mail each other snack baskets.

378 Try science experiments that are safe to do at home.

379 Go to a local tourist attraction.

380 Go to a place of worship.

381 Carve pumpkins together.

382 Go to a vintage record store.

383 Get matching bracelets/bands.

384 Wear as many clothes as possible and then help each other take them off.

1000 Bucket List Ideas for Couple

385 Have a staring contest.

386 Buy weird Halloween costumes.

387 Learn to pronounce difficult words correctly.

388 Go to a comic-con.

389 Get plain white caps and decorate hats for each other.

390 Debate regarding the existence of aliens.

391 Walk around at 3 AM to admire the city.

392 Sit in your car and talk for hours.

393 Watch inspiring TedTalk videos.

394 Have a Minecraft date.

395 Give each other a kiss for every airplane you see.

396 Discuss how different your lives would be if you never met.

397 Go to a clothing store and pick an outfit for each other.

398 Oil each other's hair.

399 Dress up as your partner's favorite fictional character.

400 Dress up as your partner's biggest fantasy.

401 Hack each other's Snapchats for a day.

402 Order a cake with your partner for no reason and eat it together.

403 Pet-sit together.

404 Make a vegan meal.

405 Instead of making multiple cookies, make one gigantic cookie!

406 Build a birdhouse.

407 Make a DIY kite by following a YouTube tutorial.

408 Make origami together.

409 Go stationery shopping.

410 Bet each other to do something embarrassing in public.

411 Buy a cheap skateboard and learn it.

412 Make a time capsule (with a letter and an object).

413 Hold a yard sale.

414 Watch an animated movie.

415 Get something from a restaurant and replicate it at home.

416 Learn the choreography of a dance routine.

417 Go on a trampoline together.

418 Crash a wedding.

419 Play UNO.

420 Get spooky and buy an Ouija board!

421 Make a silly movie with your partner.

422 Follow DIY skincare hacks together.

423 Try the Gigi Hadid pasta!

424 Watch cartoons that you both enjoyed as kids.

425 Do TikTok's PowerPoint Night! Choose a fun/funny topic to present a PowerPoint on.

426 Have a popcorn fight.

427 Try a new skincare item together.

428 Develop a skincare routine together.

429 Practice stand-up comedy with each other.

430 Play ping-pong.

431 Kiss each other unexpectedly.

432 Develop inside jokes.

433 Get each other customized stickers.

434 Get LED lights for your bedroom.

435 Review a movie/song.

436 Join the mile-high club!

437 Send voice notes.

438 Teach children together.

439 Take a Pilates class.

440 Buy popcorn and add your favorite seasonings to it.

441 Walk around a store, buy something random and use it.

442 Play games from your childhood.

443 Play a board game but induce an 18+ theme (e.g., stripping!)

444 Find an affordable place to eat with fantastic food and be regulars.

445 Pretend you're models/movie stars and take pictures of each other.

446 Make a music video together.

447 Throw a private party in the woods.

448 Write a fake name and an auto-generated number from a text application at a gas station bathroom and see who calls.

449 Watch a movie in a foreign language.

450 Prank your partner's parents together.

451 Buy a dinner set.

452 Try Dulce de Leche chocolate bars.

453 Have a trip to El Dorado.

454 Watch a live UEFA Champions League match.

455 Sing the UEFA Champions League anthem together.

456 Go to a World Cup game.

457 Learn archery.

458 Send your partner to get something from a store that doesn't exist and see their reaction.

459 Visit Japan, preferably during the Sakura season.

460 See Milky Way in a completely dark area.

461 Have a conversation about religion.

462 Debate about the existence of an alternate universe.

463 Have breakfast items all day.

464 Go on a Rickshaw ride.

465 Replace promise rings with engagement rings.

466 Get a pet fish and name him.

467 Shower each other with kisses.

468 Try sensual food items (e.g., oysters).

469 Visit a beach during turtle hatching season.

470 Name your plushy.

471 Have your own handshake.

472 Have your own version of the pinky promise.

473 Take an online course together.

474 Do photography.

475 Do laundry together.

476 Look at old Facebook statuses together.

477 Have a conversation about your exes.

478 Do something special on your monthly anniversary.

479 Make soup when your partner has a cold.

480 Warm each other's hands when it's cold.

481 Tease each other.

482 Make out in the cinema.

483 Put henna on your partner's hands.

484 Get temporary tattoos.

485 Ask your better half to be your Valentine even if you have been together for a while.

486 Buy each other a gift on Valentine's.

487 Hold each other's hand during a scary movie.

488 Try each other's comfort foods.

489 Try each other's ramen recipes.

490 Talk about your triggers.

491 Talk about your traumas.

492 Set a safe word.

493 Talk about your turn ons.

494 Talk about your turn offs.

495 Get essential oils.

496 Reassure your partner whenever they need reassurance.

497. Put each other's number on speed dial.

498. Save your partner's name with an emoji.

499. Set your partner's picture as your WhatsApp wallpaper.

500. Set boundaries.

501. Purchase a clay kit and get creative.

502. Put your partner's initials in your bios.

503. Watch a confusing movie (e.g., Tenet)

504. Watch a movie with an open ending and discuss the ambiguous ending.

505 Play soccer with a plastic bottle.

506 Talk about your childhoods.

507 Feed each other food.

508 Learn how to make spun sugar.

509 Share cotton candy.

510 Make out in a public bathroom.

511 Be your partner's number 1 fan.

512 Go on a sushi date.

513 Comment on your partner's pictures on social media.

514 Ask each other questions from "Are You Smarter than A 5th Grader".

515 Sleep on top of each other.

516 Kiss each other for hours.

517 Try new sleeping positions.

518 Try everything on a restaurant's menu.

519 Travel with other couples.

520 Celebrate a religious festival.

521 Try intermittent fasting.

522 Propose to each other with a ring pop.

523 Touch your partner's butt in public.

524 Make each other wholesome memes.

525 Play your version of "A Minute to Win It."

526 Donate blood together.

527 Add your partner to your family's WhatsApp group.

528 Give your partner your shirt for when you're away.

529 Try a food item together that you've always been scared to eat.

530 Start a blog where you both share reviews of restaurants.

531 Rent a projector and have your own drive-in movie!

532 Heat the hot water bottle when your partner has period cramps.

533 Have a drawer full of snacks for you and your partner.

534 Finish a whole ice cream tub together.

535 Ask about each other's mental health.

536 Tell your partner how much you love them.

537 Have a warm bath together with rose petals.

538 Leave cute post-it notes for each other.

539 Get an electric scalp massager and use it on each other.

540 Get some romantic scented candles.

541 Write a cheesy caption on social media about your partner.

542 Take cute kissing pictures/videos.

543 Write a song for each other – Phoebe Buffay style!

544 Share cute notes when you have to be away.

545 Share earphones.

546 Remember your partner's menstruation date and get them chocolates before their period starts.

547 Send customized cards on holidays.

548 Share your fantasies.

549 Go to a football screening together.

550 Bet on small things and set penalties.

551 Rant to each other.

552 Use Joey Tribbiani's "I was backpacking across Western Europe" on your partner.

553 Have your own The Perks of Being a Wallflower inspired "infinite moment."

554 Make a wish at the Trevi Fountain.

555 Make melted crayon art.

556 Breathe in helium balloons.

557 Move-in together.

558 Feed homeless people.

559 Decide on a direction and walk in a straight line, climb over anything that gets in the way; whoever gets the farthest wins!

560 Kiss each other on New Year's at midnight.

561 Nap at the airport together while traveling.

562 Eat at Nusr-et together.

563 Paint rocks together.

564 Try new pickup lines on each other.

565 Tell each other exaggerated stories! The most outrageous story wins.

566 Sit by the lake/swimming pool and hold each other's hand.

567 Follow a cooking tutorial... in another language with no subtitles!

568 Get a hammock.

569 Rent a Telescope.

570 Go to Chinatown or a place dedicated to a particular race.

571 Learn the sign language together.

572 Teach your partner your hobby and vice-versa.

573 Attend a free lecture at a university.

574 Research the history of your town together.

575 Visit a cool and cheap taco place.

576 Walk around your local town center and mess around in the stores.

577 Go to see an exhibit for something you both barely know anything about.

578 Download Draw Something and play together.

579 If you're away, have a Discord music date!

580 Go to a restaurant with live music.

581 Go on Google Earth and show each other places you want to travel to.

582 Make smoothies.

583 Play Frisbee on the beach.

584 Have a Call of Duty date.

585 Play Just Dance.

586 Take candid pictures of each other.

587 Get matching robes.

588 Have a TikTok date.

589 Make tea and have an all English breakfast.

590 Buy lots of snacks and binge eat.

591 Cover a song together – even if you both can't sing!

592 Have a trip to the local adult store!

593 Have a fancy tea party.

594 Play Pokémon together.

595 Get rolled ice cream.

596 Have a day dedicated to your partner.

597 Get a local map out and throw dice at it to find your destination.

598 Get matching onesies/pajamas.

599 Take each other for a haircut.

600 Look through each other's old yearbooks.

601 Take a dance class together.

602 Watch Oscar-winning movies and share your thoughts with each other.

603 Go to Winter Wonderland.

604 Have a snow fight, and then warm each other up!

605 Make pumpkin spice latte at home.

606 Imitate Gordon Ramsay together.

607 Do footsies under the table at a restaurant.

608 Get a tarot card reading done.

609 Join survey websites and earn together.

610 Ride a train together.

611 Organize a potluck dinner with your friends.

612 Write down the goals you want to achieve together.

613 Share your "happy place" with your partner.

614 Have a BBQ cookout either at your place or on the beach.

615 Get tanned together.

616 Make an album of your risqué pictures.

617 Snuggle up on the plane together.

618 Indulge in some mild PDA!

619 Watch Black Mirror: Bandersnatch and decide which direction to go in together.

620 Make new friends.

621 Go on a drive when it's raining.

622 Make a cocktail at home.

623 Take artistic pictures.

624 Dance to Christmas music together.

625 Kiss each other before work.

626 Watch a concert recording.

627 Swim in the ocean.

628 Feed each other food without using your hands.

629 Meet at the Met steps – Gossip Girl style!

630 Solve a virtual escape room.

631 Count all the moles your partner has.

632 Kiss all the moles your partner has.

633 Do the "Helpless Baker Challenge".

634 Have a date night in your SUV/truck.

635 Put a rose in your partner's hair.

636 Tuck your partner's hair behind their ear.

637 Listen to romantic music.

638 Go to a flower exhibition.

639 Get your partner a gift card.

640 Make your partner feel safe.

641 Watch the "Before" trilogy.

642 Watch Friends together.

643 Make stick food together.

644 Join fun Discord servers together.

645 If you're away, order the same meal online.

646 Make a joint playlist on Groovy.

647 Visit as many people as you can together in one night.

648 Go for a drive but only make right-hand turns. If you get stuck, turn around and make left-hand turns.

1000 Bucket List Ideas for Couple

649 Write fiction together.

650 Compare hand sizes together.

651 Walk around the city at night and then search for a place to eat at dawn.

652 Go on a drive with the passenger blindfolded, choosing random directions.

653 Dress up as pirates.

654 Go on a search for climbing trees.

655 Watch a film you have never seen before, mute it and improvise the dialogues.

656 Dress up as superheroes and stop one petty crime (e.g. littering).

657 Go to the airport and get the cheapest departing flight to anywhere and stay there for a weekend.

658 Act silly in front of the security cameras.

659 Have a breakfast picnic.

660 Go on a train ride and jump off whenever you both get bored.

661 Go indoor skydiving.

662 Swim with the dolphins.

663 Wrap a snake around your necks!

664 Bathe elephants together.

665 Have a frog jumping competition.

666 Hold monkeys together.

667 Feed an ostrich together.

668 Adopt a star for your partner.

669 Name a star after your partner.

670 Learn the national anthem of another country.

671 Ride a carriage.

672 Play matchmaker! Set up your friend with a friend of your partner's.

673 Spend a day with your partner's parents without your partner being present.

674 Leave your partner a cute note with lipstick on the bathroom mirror.

675 Make recycled paper together.

676 Create fire without any matches together.

677 Sew something for your partner.

678 Build something for your partner.

679 Learn calligraphy.

680 Make a new perfume by mixing the ones you both own.

681 Host a murder mystery dinner.

682 Dance at a party together.

683 Organize a Halloween heist – Brooklyn Nine-Nine style!

684 Visit the Madame Tussauds and pose for pictures with the wax statues.

685 Organize a cruise dinner for your partner.

686 Read a book before watching the movie.

687 Call your partner with their full name and see their reaction.

688 Ask your partner which celebrity they remind you of.

689 Buy a scent for each other.

690 Take a mud bath.

691 Eat with chopsticks for a whole day.

692 Order room service.

693 Sell things that you both no longer need.

694 Get a cookbook and cook every recipe on it.

695 Create a new ice cream flavor by mixing your favorite ones.

696 Drink juice from a fresh coconut.

697 Have a complete carnivore diet a whole weekend.

698 Only have raw food for a day.

699 Go to one of those pitch-black restaurants.

700 Host an "only desserts" party.

701 Grow herbs together.

702 Pretend your partner is a celebrity in public and ask for their autograph.

703 Build a house with cards.

704 Play games with strangers online.

705 Do crossword puzzles.

706 Google each other's name.

707 Do a juggling competition.

708 Blow balloons together and see who can blow the most.

709 Kiss each other under the mistletoe.

710 Sing cringe songs together.

711 Help your partner recreate their childhood pictures.

712 Have a "Who Can Stay up the Longest" contest.

713 Take a picture underwater.

714 Offer your partner their favorite skittles.

715 Get your partner their favorite chocolates.

716 Be extra nice to your partner when they are menstruating.

717 Have a "Who Can Stay Quiet the Longest" contest.

718 Find the meaning of your names together.

719 Learn how to give CPR together.

720 Buy a place that you both want to grow old in.

721 Have a sundae on a Sunday.

722 Find out your sun, moon, and rising stars together.

723 Learn the lyrics to a foreign song.

724 Learn "I Love You" in 10 different languages.

725 Tell each other what you love the most about the other person.

726 Tell each other what you find annoying about the other person.

727 Send flowers to your partner's workplace.

728 Make noodles from scratch together.

729. Learn how to tap dance.

730. Ride a hover board together.

731. Visit a rainforest.

732. Get matching henna tattoos.

733. See the fountains dancing at The Dubai Fountain.

734. Spend a night in a haunted house.

735. Go on a trip with your partner's parents.

736. Visit the Hollywood Walk of Fame.

737 Take a picture of your partner with their favorite celebrities' stars at the Hollywood Walk of Fame.

738 Watch Game of Thrones together.

739 Learn how to hula dance.

740 See the Niagara Falls together.

741 Visit Bahamas' Pink Sands Beach.

742 Visit France's Pont des Arts Bridge.

743 Float with each other in the Dead Sea.

744 Visit the Van Gogh museum together.

745 Celebrate the Holi festival together.

746 Attend Spain's La Tomatina festival.

747 Talk only through song lyrics for a day.

748 Get matching socks.

749 Look at your birth charts together.

750 Decorate a Christmas tree together.

751 Visit a new place each New Year's.

752 Ride the London Eye.

753 Get matching bucket hats.

754 Share a drink with two straws.

755 Get a whiteboard and leave cute messages for your partner.

756 Ride a scary rollercoaster.

757 Write a letter to each other to be opened in the future.

758 Create a hashtag for you and your partner.

759 Stalk your exes together!

760 Make a vision board together.

761 Get those "Mr. & Mrs." Mugs.

762 Try edible bugs.

763 Have fondue together.

764 Tell your mutual friends that you both are getting married (or having a baby) and see their reaction.

765 Ask your partner when they realized that they were in love with you.

766 Introduce your partner as "My Future Husband/Wife."

767 Find ways to tell each other that you love each other without saying "I Love You".

768 Write "I Love You" by arranging rose petals.

769 Go to a burlesque show.

770 Make a DIY gift for your partner.

771 Make a Christmas playlist together.

772 Make hot chocolate bombs.

773 Watch holiday movies.

774 Make your own advent calendar together.

775 Get a haircut of your partner's choice.

776 Pop a zit for your partner.

777 Massage your partner's head/back if they have a headache/backache.

778 Make chili together.

779 Make curry together.

780 Bring a snack for your partner when they are busy working.

781 Awaken your inner child together and try catching raindrops on your tongue.

782 Give your partner a forehead kiss.

783 Write thank you letters to your mutual friends.

784 Make a DIY snow globe for your partner.

785 Witness the Changing of the Guard in London.

786 Get fish pedicures together.

787 Try fly-boarding together.

788 Watch Marvel movies.

789 Watch DC movies.

790 Discuss whether you prefer DC or Marvel.

791 Visit all seven continents.

792 Visit all the wonders of the world.

793 Visit The Catacombs in Paris – a place filled with bones and skulls.

794 Ride a gondola in Venice.

795 Attend the Burning Man festival.

796 Ride swan boats.

797 Ride a kiddie train together.

798 Make dumplings from scratch.

799 Prank your friends that you have broken up and see their reaction.

800 Ask about your partner's school life.

801 Ask your significant other about the last time they cried.

802 Make samosas together.

803 Tell your partner that you are grateful for them.

804 Watch the sunrise and sunset in one day with your partner.

805 Make bread together.

806 Write a haiku for your partner.

807 Learn a magic trick together.

808 Jam to Pewdiepie's T-Series diss track.

809 Buy your partner their favorite celebrity's merch.

810 DIY Kylie Jenner's Valentine's Day flowers for your partner.

811 Invest in the stock market.

812 Buy a lottery ticket together.

813 Buy something cheap on Wish together.

814 Try Chrissy Teigen's recipes.

815 Make a DIY flower staircase with your partner.

816 Remind your partner to drink more water.

817 Make DIY wall décor.

818 Go shopping in Thailand together.

819 Make a DIY flower mirror with your partner.

820 Steal your boyfriend's old clothes.

821 Make your old outfits look new again by following YouTube tutorials together.

822 Eat at the worst rated restaurant in your city.

823 Remind your partner to keep their phones with them before they leave for work.

824 Keep painkillers with yourself in case your partner ever needs them.

825 Play "4 Pics 1 Word" together.

826 Revisit your childhood video games.

827 Have a Molten chocolate lava cake.

828 Book the tickets to your partner's favorite band/singer.

829 Remember your partner's close relatives' names.

830 Spray your partner's scent on your pillow when they are away.

831 Ask how your partner's day was.

832 Get your partner a cute mask.

833. Ask your partner if you need to improve yourself in any way.

834. Ask your partner if you've ever said something that hurt them.

835. Work on yourself for your partner.

836. Appreciate your better half for the little things they do.

837. Take your partner's side.

838. Be kind to your partner.

839. Apologize when you do something wrong.

840. Browse for Valentine's Day's couple offers before going out.

841 Have a red velvet cake with your partner on Valentine's Day.

842 Don't make a promise that you can't keep.

843 Get a facial done together.

844 Make fresh juice together.

845 Learn to surf together.

846 Watch Takashi's castle.

847 Have a food eating competition.

848 Visit a farm with your better half.

849 Collect eggs from the hens at the farm.

850 Do something that you're both doing for the first time.

851 Make a mug cake with your partner.

852 Listen to Taylor Swift's old and latest version of "Love Story".

853 Do a ropes course.

854 Go to a park with your partner and pick up the litter together.

855 Participate in a race.

856 Attend a wedding of someone from another religion.

857 Have a fun night in Vegas.

858 Get a Thai massage together.

859 Ride a camel together.

860 Learn new things together.

861 Learn Taekwondo together.

862 See an NBA game live.

863 Watch a Dolphin show with your partner.

864 Play fighting.

865 Respect your partner's family and friends.

866 Save posts on the internet that you think will be helpful to your partner.

867 Proofread your partner's work.

868 Be your partner "shoulder to cry on".

869 Send "anonymous hugs" to your partner through Twitter bots.

870 Celebrate a white Christmas with your partner.

871 Learn how to tango.

872 Read happy love stories.

873. Read tragic love stories.

874. See Big Ben with your partner.

875. Thrift a designer outfit together.

876. Fly first class together.

877. Visit a castle.

878. Watch Bridgerton together.

879. Have turns doing a flip on a trampoline.

880. Take one picture every day for a year.

881 Read magazines together.

882 Sleep on a single bed together.

883 Sleep on the couch together.

884 Cover your partner with a blanket if they fall asleep.

885 Help your partner take their makeup off after a long day.

886 Make DIY bird feeders.

887 Get COVID tests done together.

888 Count stars.

889 Visit a village.

890 Tickle each other.

891 Dedicate a song to your significant other at an open bar.

892 Take a tandem bike ride with your partner.

893 Put your partner's phone on charge after a long day.

894 Restock your partner's favorite snacks.

895 Do things with your partner that they never had a chance to do as a kid.

896 Carve your names on a tree.

897 Attempt to do SFX makeup together.

898 Open a tight jar for your partner.

899 Sing a song but in the worst way possible.

900 Make each other laugh.

901 Rub your noses together while kissing.

902 Kiss in a cinema.

903 Kiss on top of a Ferris wheel (like in Love, Simon).

904 Participate in a paintball gunfight together.

905 Have a water fight on a double date.

906 Learn each other's favorite board game.

907 Go to an open mic couples' night and get on stage unprepared.

908 Do a Harry Potter marathon.

909 Do a Lord of the Rings marathon.

910 Take a pottery class together.

911 Try a goat yoga session together.

912 Go to a food festival and have a couples' Mukbang.

913. Read your significant other their favorite book.

914. Sleep in your partner's lap.

915. Go see a live play together.

916. Go to an opera show.

917. Visit a popular psychic together for fun.

918. Tell each other about the cringiest moment in your relationship.

919. Introduce each other to your family.

920. Buy indoor plants and name them together.

921 Go on a sugar cleanse together.

922 Go on an alcohol detox.

923 Visit a chiropractor and get your bodies professionally cracked.

924 Make free meals together for the poor.

925 Plant a tree together every month for a year.

926 Go on a scavenger hunt together.

927 Spend a day in a countryside hotel together.

928 Milk a cow for the first time together.

929 Call each other by the name of your favorite desserts for one day.

930 See Kevin Hart perform live.

931 Go on Ellen together.

932 Go to a thrift shop together.

933 Go to a jazz club together.

934 Play laser tag together.

935 Learn how to canoe together.

936 Spoon feed each other.

937 Buy your partner flowers after they've had a long day.

938 Reenact a scene out of your favorite movie.

939 Watch iconic 90s movies together.

940 Have a PJ day.

941 Play charades together.

942 Make a couples' scrapbook together.

943 Blow bubbles in the park.

944 Play hide and seek around the house.

945 Go up to a random person together, ask them what year this is, then look at each other and yell "We did it!"

946 Play video games with each other.

947 Make snow angels together.

948 Have a pillow fight.

949 Go on a chocolate factory tour together.

950 Do the bottle flip challenge together – first to land 5 wins!

951 Do the 'my boyfriend does my makeup' challenge.

952 Let your partner do your hair.

953 Play the egg roulette game.

954 Do the Kylie Jenner lip challenge, and take ridiculous pictures with the results.

955 Ride bicycles around the town together.

956 Laugh until you cry with your partner.

957 Be a part of a flash mob.

958 Write song for each other.

959 Write poetry for each other.

960 Go crazy on a trampoline together.

961 Learn a new language together.

962 Learn salsa together.

963 Go to a paper lantern festival with your partner.

964 Be woken up with a kiss.

965 Hold hands while you sleep.

966 Hug each other to sleep.

967 Lay your head against your partner's chest, and listen to their heartbeat.

968 Wash your car together.

969 Pick a car both of you love, and go buy it together.

970 Build a DIY pool together.

971 Host a dance party.

972 Tie your hoodies together for an hour.

973 Record a duet singing performance.

974 Order for each other at the restaurant.

975 Have your partner paint your nails.

976 Spend a night sleeping by a campfire.

977 Go for romantic evening walks together.

978 Throw your pet a giant birthday party.

979 Sponsor one of your partner's shopping sprees.

980 Buy your partner something they've been wanting for a while.

981 Cuddle and tell each other everything you're grateful for.

982 Wear matching outfits.

983 Start a small business together.

984 Go fishing together.

985 Drive around randomly and explore your city.

986 Pick a subject you're both into, and take classes together.

987 Learn how to surf together.

988 Take tango classes together.

989 Attend a live TedTalk together.

990 Go see a circus together.

991 Take a picture every day of the year, and compile all 365 pictures into a video.

992 Try a couples' hypnotherapy session.

993 Do the 23andme test together and find out your ancestral roots.

994 Leave cute post-it notes around the house for your partner to find.

995 Tell each other 'I love you' in a different language every day.

996 Say what you like the most about each other.

997 Say five things you both appreciate about your bond.

998 Thank each other for the amazing love you've shared over the years.

999 Start working on your next 1000-ideas bucket list together.

1000 Promise each other to stay together for the rest of your lives.

Reference List:

1. https://fullylived.com/social-bucket-list-ideas/

2. https://bucketlistjourney.net/couples-bucket-list-things-to-do/

3. https://www.pinterest.ph/briluyando/couples-bucket-list/

4. https://www.pinterest.com.au/jessicas2947/together/
   (Collection by Jessica Scott)

www.ingramcontent.com/pod-product-compliance
Lightning Source LLC
Chambersburg PA
CBHW071457070526
44578CB00001B/370